2 Timothy

Thoroughly Equipped for Every Good Work

Other Titles in the Book by Book Video Bible Study Series:

GENESIS
Video Bible Studies with Richard Bewes, Paul Blackham and special guest Anne Graham-Lotz.
Accompanying Study Guide by Paul Blackham

EXODUS
Video Bible Studies with Richard Bewes, Paul Blackham and special guest Joseph Steinberg.
Accompanying Study Guide by Paul Blackham

PSALMS 20–29
Video Bible Studies with Richard Bewes, Paul Blackham and special guest Stephen Lungu.
Accompanying Study Guide by Paul Blackham

GALATIANS
Video Bible Studies with Richard Bewes, Paul Blackham and special guest Jonathan Edwards.
Accompanying Study Guide by Paul Blackham

JONAH
Video Bible Studies with Richard Bewes, Paul Blackham and special guest George Verwer.
Accompanying Study Guide by Paul Blackham

1 PETER
Video Bible Studies with Richard Bewes, Paul Blackham and special guest Don Carson.
Accompanying Study Guide by Paul Blackham

THE GOSPEL OF JOHN
Video Bible Studies with Richard Bewes, Paul Blackham and special guest Anne Graham-Lotz.
Accompanying Study Guide by Paul Blackham

1 & 2 TESSALONIANS
Video Bible Studies with Richard Bewes, Paul Blackham and special guest Rico Tice.
Accompanying Study Guide by Paul Blackham

JAMES
Video Bible Studies with Richard Bewes, Paul Blackham and special guest Jonathon Edwards.
Accompanying Study Guide by Paul Blackham

2 Timothy

Thoroughly Equipped for Every Good Work

Authentic
LIFESTYLE

11 10 09 08 07 06 05   7 6 5 4 3 2 1

First published in 2005 by Authentic Media
9 Holdom Avenue, Bletchley, Milton Keynes, MK1 1QR, UK
and
P.O. Box 1047, Waynesboro, GA 30830–2047, USA

Website: www.authenticmedia.co.uk

British Library Cataloguing in Publication Data
A catalogue record for this book is available from the British Library

ISBN 1–85078–569-4

Cover Design by Diane Bainbridge
Typeset by WestKey Ltd, Falmouth, Cornwall
Print Management by Adare Carwin
Printed and Bound by J. H. Haynes & Co. Ltd., Sparkford

Richard and Liz Bewes, thank your for 22 years
of wonderful leadership, service and vision at
All Souls Church, London, England

Contents

Contents

How To Use This Book

BOOK BY BOOK is a video-based Bible Study resource with linked Bible Study questions and a mini-commentary, provided in this Study Guide by the Rev'd Dr Paul Blackham. It has been designed principally for use in small groups, but can also be used for personal study or larger group situations.

Structure of Video and Study Guide:

There is a strong link between the video-based Bible discussions and the written Study Guide to help group discussion and study. Key features provided by the studies are as follows:

- There are 6 x programmes on the video.
- Each programme is 15 minutes long.
- The on-screen host is Richard Bewes, with co-host Paul Blackham. A specially invited guest joins them in the Bible discussions.
- Questions from the video-based discussions are printed at the start of each section of the Study Guides.
- In the Study Guide, there are also Bible Study questions on a selected portion of the text covered in each session. These focus on one short Biblical passage in greater detail.
- There is no 'answer guide' to the questions in the Study Guide – although clearly answers (and applications for daily living as Christians) are provided to questions posed during the on-screen discussions. Answers may also be found in the Further Notes at the back of the Guide.
- The Daily Readings after each Bible Study are intended to give the reader a broader picture of what is going on in each part of the Bible covered in a session.
- There are more detailed notes on each session at the back of the Study Guide. These will be of great help to leaders or anyone wanting to learn more about the particular book of the Bible. (This could also be used in isolation from the on-screen discussions as a mini-commentary.) Further questions are listed at the end of each session.

These are generally more difficult and are possibly of most use to those who would like to study the relevant passages in more detail.

Structure of Group Session:

Please note – the material has been designed in such a way that there is no need for a specially trained leader in order to be able to use the material.

- We would highly recommend that each group member reads the relevant Bible passage prior to your discussion.
- Timing: we estimate that the study session will take about 1 hour. Given the volume of material you may even choose to take two weeks per study – using the questions linked to the video discussions for one week and the Bible Study questions for the next.
- Use of the video programme: for many, simply watching the discussion of the Bible passage may in itself be a wonderful encouragement and learning tool, and your study session may be limited to discussion on this alone. It is entirely up to your group as to whether you watch the on-screen study before or after your own group Bible Study on the passage.
- Prayer: you may want to include personal applications in your group prayer time which arise from the discussions.

Some introductory thoughts from Paul Blackham:

Thousands of small groups are starting up all over the world – but what is it that is going to sustain them? It has to be the Bible. However, so often people don't quite know what to do with these small groups. Meeting together, sharing testimonies and experiences or the odd verse is ultimately too sparse a diet to sustain people's spiritual needs in the long run and really help them to grow.

What is needed is confidence in the Bible, and the ability to be able to go to a book of the Bible rather than just an isolated verse. Each book of the Bible was written with a purpose, and it is only really as we digest it as a book that we understand the real message, purpose, direction, storyline and characters.

It's a lot easier than people often think. You might think, "Oh, I can't manage a whole book of the Bible", but what we're trying to do in BOOK BY BOOK is to break it down and show that actually it's easy.

The Bible was written not for specialists, not for academics – it was written for the regular believers, down the ages.

Introduction to the Book of 2 Timothy

2 Timothy is possibly the very last letter that the great apostle Paul ever wrote. We come to the end of the thrilling life of a man who had served Jesus with all his heart, mind, soul and strength. What would be his final instruction to the Church? It is clear that this letter was written when Paul was a prisoner (see 1:8, 16). As he got ready to die, what did he want to say in order to build up the expanding multinational Church of Jesus the Messiah?

In our day we see the desperate need for Bible teachers in every local church. We have seen the terrible devastation brought on the Church by false teachers, self-serving personalities, status-seeking careerists and men who do little more than declare their own religious opinions from the pulpit. In this final letter from Paul we see how his greatest concern for the health and growth of the future Church was to see self-sacrificial Bible teachers who were determined to speak only as God has spoken.

In the first letter to Timothy Paul instructed Timothy in all the basics of being a faithful minister in a local church. In this second letter he sets two alternatives before Timothy. He could be a barren, compromised, unfaithful minister who would be ashamed at the appearing of Jesus; or he could be a fruitful and faithful minister who would be received with great joy by Jesus on that final day. It is a vital challenge. Having been united to Jesus in His death and resurrection, what kind of life and ministry will we have? How can we fulfil our duty in the way that Paul himself did? If we are saved from hell but live a life of fruitless compromise, how will we face Jesus when He appears? Just what did He save us for?

Video Questions

Session 1

2 Timothy 1:1-7
Paul and Timothy

The following are the questions featured in the video which accompanies this Study Guide. If you wish to, you or your group can use them to recap on what you have been watching. Following this, there is a Bible study on a section of the passage covered by this session which can be used instead or additionally.

Key Truth: Paul writes to Timothy to encourage him to remain a faithful Bible teacher, living by the Spirit and holding to the promise of life.

1. The Promise of Life (verses 1–2)

What do we know about the author of this letter and the situation in which it was written?

Paul the apostle went through so many difficulties to share the gospel and build up the Church. What was it that sustained him through this demanding ministry?

2. Paul remembers Timothy (verses 3–5)

Why does Paul write what could have been his last letter to Timothy? What is his main concern for the Church?

What do we learn about Timothy's family background, and how can this be an encouragement to us today?

3. Paul reminds Timothy (verses 6–7)

What is the 'gift of God' mentioned in verse 6?

Why does Timothy need to be **reminded** of these things, verse 6? Surely he knew them already?

What do we learn about the Holy Spirit from Paul's description of Him in verse 7?

Bible Study 1

2 Timothy 1:1-7

Read 2 Timothy 1:1-14.

- When you are going through hard times what keeps you going?

- How do you think Timothy was feeling before he received this letter? What pressures was he facing? (Look at 1:8,12; 2:3,8-10; 2:25; 3:12-13; 4:2-3)

- Why then does Paul mention 'the promise of life' in verse 1?

- How often do you think about Jesus' return and our future glory in the New Creation? How can you make this truth more central to your life?

- In verses 3-5 Paul mentions two 'chains' of people. How does Timothy fit into each? How does this form the basis for verse 6? (cf. 2 Timothy 2:2)

- In verse 7 three aspects of the Holy Spirit's work are mentioned. Thinking of Timothy's situation and verses 8-14, why does Paul highlight these three?

- How can you use 2 Timothy 1:1-7 as you pray a) for yourself, b) for your church leaders? Then pray!

Daily Readings

Day 1:   Deuteronomy 30:11–20

Day 2:   Joshua chapter 1

Day 3:   Psalm 21

Day 4:   Isaiah chapter 61

Day 5:   John chapter 14

Day 6:   2 Peter chapter 3

Day 7:   Revelation chapter 1

Session 2

2 Timothy 1:8-14
A Herald and a Guardian

The following are the questions featured in the video which accompanies this Study Guide. If you wish to, you or your group can use them to recap on what you have been watching. Following this, there is a Bible study on a section of the passage covered by this session which can be used instead or additionally.

Key Truth: Timothy must follow the pattern set by Jesus and Paul, teaching and suffering for the gospel of life.

1. Suffer Without Shame (verse 8)

In verse 8, Paul calls Timothy to suffer for the gospel. Surely suffering is an 'optional extra' to our faith – dependant on where or when we live?

2. Life and Immortality in Jesus (verses 9-10)

How can we be sure that we will receive the grace and help of God through our suffering? How do we know that we don't have to be ashamed?

3. Paul Suffers Without Shame (verses 11-12)

In verse 11, Paul says he was appointed a 'herald, an apostle and a teacher' of the gospel. When was he appointed to do these things and what do they mean?

There's some talk here about 'guarding' – in verse 12 and verse 14. What is it that Timothy has to guard, and why?

4. 'He Guards... You Guard' (verses 12–14)

What do you think is this 'pattern of sound teaching', or brief outline of teaching that is mentioned in verse 13?

We so often see theology as being a very separate part of our Christian lives to things like faith and love. What does verse 13 have to say about that?

Bible Study 2

2 Timothy 1:8–14

- Think of a time when you were ashamed to testify about Jesus or Paul. What made you nervous or ashamed?

- Read verses 8–14. What four commands does Paul give Timothy? Why therefore must all Church leaders follow Paul's example and teaching?

- Why might someone be ashamed of Jesus or Paul (verses 8 and 11–12)?

- In verse 12 Paul gives two reasons why he is not ashamed. What are they? How do verses 9–10 give credibility to these reasons?

- Which of these truths do you especially need to be convinced of so that you will not be ashamed in the future? Pray about this.

- From what we have seen already in 2 Timothy, how is the gospel to be guarded? What is God's role and what is ours?

- What can you do in your church so that verse 13 is better obeyed?

Daily Readings

Day 1:   Deuteronomy 32:1–47

Day 2:   Daniel chapter 3

Day 3:   Psalm 69

Day 4:   Isaiah chapter 62

Day 5:   Mark 8:27–38

Day 6:   1 Peter chapter 1

Day 7:   Revelation 2:8–11

Session 3

2 Timothy 1:15–2:14
Desertion and Endurance

The following are the questions featured in the video which accompanies this Study Guide. If you wish to, you or your group can use them to recap on what you have been watching. Following this, there is a Bible study on a section of the passage covered by this session which can be used instead or additionally.

Key Truth: For Timothy to bear fruit and eternal glory, he must work hard by God's grace and keep passing the gospel on to others.

1. 'Everyone' Deserted Me (1:15)

What do we learn from the mention of these 3 men at the end of chapter 1? Phygelus, Hermogenes and Onesiphorus?

2. Be Strong, Endure, Compete and Work Hard (2:1–6)

What do we learn about the chain of responsibility in verse 2?

What is involved in teaching the Bible?

3. Reflect, Remember and Remind (2:7–14)

Paul tells Timothy to reflect, remember and remind. Why is so important that he gives time to thinking about the gospel as well as living it out?

What do we need to remember?

Were verses 11–13 a hymn or a creedal statement?

Verse 14 contains a warning about quarrelling over words. Doesn't this seem a little harsh?

Bible Study 3

2 Timothy 1:15-2:14

- How do verses 15-18 fit into the context of chapter 1? Why does Paul start chapter 2 with 'You then...'?

- In what way does 2:2 explain how 1:13-14 are to be obeyed?

- What type of people is Timothy to train? Given the context why are these qualities necessary?

- If you are a Church leader, who are you training in this way? If you are not a leader what can you do to give your leaders the necessary time and resources?

- What will life be like if you are committed to this (2:3-10)? Use the words in this passage to describe the normal Christian life.

- What are the challenges of the three illustrations in verses 4-6?

- In verses 8-14 what does Timothy need to remember and remind others about? How does each truth encourage and challenge us?

- What is the warning to churches where these truths are not constantly taught?

- Spend time praying for your church.

Daily Readings

Day 1:   Exodus chapter 18

Day 2:   Daniel chapter 6

Day 3:   Psalm 145

Day 4:   Isaiah chapter 63

Day 5:   Mark 6:7–30

Day 6:   Hebrews 12:1–13

Day 7:   Revelation 3:7–13

Session 4

2 Timothy 2:15-3:9
Correctly Handling the Word of Truth

The following are the questions featured in the video which accompanies this Study Guide. If you wish to, you or your group can use them to recap on what you have been watching. Following this, there is a Bible study on a section of the passage covered by this session which can be used instead or additionally.

Key Truth: False teaching and godless living is deadly and can only be countered as Timothy flees evil and pursues the Biblical faith and lifestyle..

1. Godly and Ungodly Speakers (2:15-18)

How do we correctly handle the Bible? What are the criteria to judge the workman's work, verse 15?

We are warned that 'godless chatter' could lead to such false teaching that destroys other peoples' faith. How? And how can we avoid it?

Thinking about verses 17–18, how seriously should we take the unorthodox teaching of a church leader?

2. God's Foundation (2:19)

Is verse 19 a direct quote from Numbers chapter 16? How does this reference help illustrate his point?

There is quite a lot of warnings and encouragements in these next verses. What do they mean?

3. Godly Living (2:20–26)

How does the rest of the chapter explain how we are to be prepared to do good work for the Master of the house?

4. The Form of Godliness (3:1– 9)

What are we to make of this long list of ungodly things in the first 9 verses of chapter 3? Why does Paul give these details?

Bible Study 4

2 Timothy 2:15–3:9

- Think about your denomination or local churches. Do you think false teachers are rare or common? Do we need to be concerned about them?

- Read through the passage then answer these four questions:

  1. What characterises a false teacher? *Wondered away from the Word.*
  2. What are the results of false teaching?
  3. What characterises an approved workman? *a workman correctly speaking the Word*
  4. What must he avoid and what must he pursue? *evil desires, the Lord's Will.*

- What does it mean to 'correctly handle the Word of Truth' (verse 15)? As much as possible answer this from 2 Timothy.

- What is the recurring theme in 3:1–5? How do these verses compare to modern society? Where do you see these attitudes infiltrating the Church?

- What can you do to counter false teaching, individually and as part of a church? What responsibility do we have for others?

- A friend comes to you concerned that her church leader could be a false teacher. What should she be on the look out for? What should she do if her fears are confirmed?

Daily Readings

Day 1:   Numbers chapter 16

Day 2:   1 Kings chapter 18

Day 3:   Psalm 95

Day 4:   Jeremiah chapter 23

Day 5:   Matthew chapter 24

Day 6:   2 Peter chapter 2

Day 7:   Revelation 2:18–29

Session 5

2 Timothy 3:10–4:8
Scriptures and Preaching

The following are the questions featured in the video which accompanies this Study Guide. If you wish to, you or your group can use them to recap on what you have been watching. Following this, there is a Bible study on a section of the passage covered by this session which can be used instead or additionally.

Key Truth: In view of Christ's appearing, Timothy's priority must be to teach the Bible, despite rejection and persecution, because only in this way will people be saved and equipped for a godly life.

1. 'My Teaching, My Way of Life' (3:10–13)

Why does Paul make a list to Timothy all about himself in verses 10–11 of chapter 3? What is it there for?

2. The Purpose of the Hebrew Scriptures (3:14– 17)

What do verses 14–17 tell us about the Bible? How should we treat it, and use it in our lives?

What does it mean that Scripture is 'God-breathed'?

3. Preach the Word (4:1–5) (cf. 2:1–6)

What do we learn in verses 3–4 of chapter 4 about sinful humanity? What is our sinful reaction to the faithful preaching of the Word?

4. Keep the Faith (4:6–8)

Can you explain why Paul describes his life as being poured out like a drink offering, as in verse 6?

Bible Study 5

2 Timothy 3:10-4:8

1. Think about the church meetings you go to. What occupies the most time? What in practice is the main focus, and why do people come?

2. In what ways do Paul's qualities, listed in verses 10 and 11, contrast with those of the false teachers?

3. Look at the comparison in verses 12–15. What is the pressure facing Timothy? What does he need to do and why?

4. 3:14– 4:2: what will be the (a) origin, (b) content and (c) purpose of authentic preaching?

5. 4:1–4: why will some church leaders not teach the Bible? Why does Timothy need to preach 'in season and out of season' and 'with great patience and careful instruction'? How can you encourage your church leaders more fully to obey Paul's charge in verse 2?

6. In churches today, what challenges are there to (a) the usefulness of ALL Scripture (verse 16), and (b) the 'sufficiency' of the Scriptures (verse 17)?

7. In 4:1 and 4:6–8 what great realities does Paul impress upon Timothy? Where have we seen these before?

8. You have been given the responsibility of choosing your new church leader. Discuss what the job description will be and how the new minister should plan his weekly timetable.

Daily Readings

Day 1:   Deuteronomy 4:1–40

Day 2:   Nehemiah chapter 8

Day 3:   Psalm 119:153–176

Day 4:   Ezekiel chapters 2–3

Day 5:   Luke 24:13–53

Day 6:   2 Peter chapter 1

Day 7:   Revelation chapter 22

Session 6

2 Timothy 4:9-4:22
Friends and Families

The following are the questions featured in the video which accompanies this Study Guide. If you wish to, you or your group can use them to recap on what you have been watching. Following this, there is a Bible study on a section of the passage covered by this session which can be used instead or additionally.

Key Truth: Our choice is between temporary comfort in this world or aligning ourselves with Paul and proclaiming the Biblical gospel, with the strength and companionship of our Lord Jesus Himself.

1. Friends

Do we perhaps see a glimpse of a weak side to the apostle Paul in the closing verses of the book? Here he is, longing for some company.

What are some of the encouraging lessons to learn from the mentioning of some of these names? Perhaps Mark, Tychicus, and others?

2. Failures

Paul also mentions quite a few 'failures' in this final section, in terms of people deserting or opposing the gospel. What are we to learn from these examples?

3. Jesus Stood By Me

How do we see the strength of Paul's faith in the Lord Jesus here, right at the end of his life?

How would you summarise the lessons of the book of 2 Timothy and what has impacted you the most?

Bible Study 6

2 Timothy 4:9-22

- The 'you' in 'grace be with you' (verse 22) is plural, meaning Paul intended the church in Ephesus to read his letter to Timothy. Why did Paul want them to do this?

- In verses 9–13 we see some who have helped Paul and others who have deserted or even harmed him. Think of the Christians you have known for the longest. Has their life and ministry become more or less like Paul's since you first knew them? Have you been helpful to them in ministry?

- Think of 2 or 3 people you will commit to encouraging, supporting and sharing what you have learnt in 2 Timothy. Resolve to start this week.

- In verse 10 why did Demas desert Paul? In what areas of your life is Satan most tempting you the same way?

- What main themes of 2 Timothy are again highlighted in verses 14–18? Where have we seen them before?

- What is Paul's mission and focus? Are these yours? If not, how do you want others to pray for you?

- Do you think you will stand firm to the end and receive the crown of righteousness? Looking back over 2 Timothy what are the main things you have learnt (a) for yourself and (b) for your church leader?

- Close by praying for each other and your church leaders.

Daily Readings

Day 1:   Genesis 35:1–15 and 48:15–16

Day 2:   1 Kings chapter 19

Day 3:   Psalm 124

Day 4:   Ezekiel chapter 34

Day 5:   John chapter 15

Day 6:   1 John 2:1–27

Day 7:   Revelation 19:1–11

Further Notes

2 Timothy 1:1-7
Paul & Timothy

Key Truth: Paul writes to Timothy to encourage him to remain a faithful Bible teacher, living by the Spirit and holding to the promise of life.

1. The Promise of Life (1:1-2)

The great apostle Paul is drawing to the end of his life. He has poured out his life in service to Jesus. He has run the race, fought the fight and laboured hard. He is just as committed to the work of the gospel as he ever was, yet it is just as costly to him as it ever was. He has been determined to bear fruit for the glory of Jesus, and that has always been a costly work.

What has sustained him through this demanding ministry?

Paul's apostolic work has been **according to the promise of life** in Jesus, verse 1. Just as Jesus was sustained by the 'joy set before Him' (Hebrews 12:1-3), so the apostle Paul had been sustained by the knowledge of the wonderful immortal life guaranteed to all who trust in Jesus. In Philippians 1:20-24 Paul admits that he would prefer to leave his body and wait in Paradise with Jesus – waiting for that unspeakably glorious resurrection when Jesus returns to earth with all the saints.

With **such** a promise of life in Jesus, we can endure just like the apostle Paul endured. Are we living for the passing life we have **now** or are we following Jesus to the **promised** life of our resurrection future? Are we pouring out our present life in order to bear fruit for eternity, or are we betraying our Saviour and Lord in compromise and selfishness?

This is the thought that Paul sets before his 'dear son' Timothy. Paul knows that the future health of the Church depends on the faithfulness of each generation of Bible teachers. Paul has such affection for Timothy because he sees how Timothy is going on in the work, grounding people in the 'grace, mercy and peace' that we have from the Father and the Son.

When Paul calls Timothy his 'son' it might mean that Paul had been instrumental in the conversion of Timothy. Paul visited Lystra on his first missionary journey (Acts 14:6–7) and Timothy may well have been one of those who heard the gospel at that time. However, we also know that Timothy had been brought up in the Scriptures by his mother and grandmother, and we would expect him to have already heard the gospel from them during his childhood years.

2. Paul Remembers Timothy (1:3–5)

Paul's concern for this next generation of Bible teachers is so strong that he constantly prays for Timothy – night and day! Paul is not exaggerating. He speaks with a clear conscience that he really has been thanking the Father for Timothy so often. As always, Paul wishes to show that he shares the same faith and practice as all the Old Testament saints, because he says that 'his forefathers' did the same in their day.

Paul remembers how Timothy wept when they last parted, and he really wants to see him again. There is nothing artificial or formal about the love Paul has for this young Bible teacher.

Timothy had enjoyed one of the very greatest privileges that anyone can know. He had grown up in a home where both his mother Lois and his grandmother Eunice were believers who loved the Hebrew Scriptures (3:15). Paul is thrilled that this third generation believer is trusting in Jesus with the best possible foundation for fruitfulness.

This is a pattern every Christian home must follow. It has been said that the first generation contends for the faith, the second generation assumes it, but the third generation denies it. Eunice and Lois had not allowed this carelessness to enter their home. Perhaps Timothy had learned to read at the family Bible studies as they had shaped his mind by the Word of God from his earliest years.

3. Paul Reminds Timothy (1:6–7)

When Paul tells Timothy what he must do, he knows that Timothy only needs to be **reminded** of these things. Paul had 'ordained' Timothy as an elder in the church by the laying on of hands (verse 6). At that time he must have set before Timothy all the duties and responsibilities that were included in that work. He must also have told him how to grow up into Christian maturity. On top of all that, Timothy had learned the Scriptures from infancy... yet he must be **reminded** of these things.

Our minds are tricky things. We have very selective memories. During the earthly ministry of Jesus we see how the disciples selectively 'forgot' whenever Jesus spoke of His death on the Cross, but they were very careful to 'remember' any teaching about the authority and glory of the Kingdom. We are all like that. Unless we are constantly reminded about the foundation truths of the gospel and Scripture we will 'forget' them. Our minds have to be constantly renewed or else our lives will never be transformed – see Romans 12:2.

So, Paul urges Timothy to 'fan into flame' the gift of God. Normally this language of 'the gift of God' would make us think about the gospel itself – Jesus, the new birth, etc. However, here, this gift is in Timothy **through** Paul laying hands on him. When we read the book of Acts we see that the Holy Spirit was given for the exercise of an office through the laying on of hands and we also see men being set aside for special service by the laying on of hands (Acts 6:6; 8:17–18; 9:17; 19:6; 1 Timothy 4:14; 5:22; Hebrews 6:2). Paul here in verse 6 seems to indicate that he had been present at Timothy's laying on of hands by the body of elders (1 Timothy 4:14). When the elders laid hands on him they were making it clear that this was the man they were setting aside for the work. Furthermore, by the laying on of hands, Timothy was reminded that it was the Holy Spirit alone who could equip him for this awesome task. In the Hebrew Scriptures men were appointed to the offices of prophet, priest and king by the anointing of oil, showing them that their job needed the power of the Holy Spirit. It seems that the act of laying on hands had a similar function in the New Testament.

Paul reminds Timothy that he has been given the gift of the Holy Spirit to equip him as a Bible teacher. Timothy must never grieve the Spirit. Rather he must strive to be more and more in harmony with the Spirit. What does the Spirit do? The Spirit's job is to bear witness to Jesus (John 15:26; 16:8–9, 14–15). What does the Spirit want? The Spirit desires the very opposite things than what our sinful nature desires (Galatians 5:16–25). Timothy must give his life as a herald of Jesus and refuse the desires of the flesh. In this way his fellowship with the Spirit will be ever deeper and stronger.

This is how Timothy will have a fruitful and faithful ministry. The Spirit will equip him to live out his union with Jesus even in this present darkness. In the power of the flesh Timothy's ministry will only be barren. In the power of the Spirit he can bear eternal fruit.

Paul makes a wonderful description of the Spirit in verse 7. The Spirit is not timid, as **we** might be in our witness to Jesus. The Holy Spirit has great power to convince and convict people of the truth of the gospel. He shares the mighty love of the Father and Son with us (see Romans 5:5) and He alone is able to give us control over the evil desires of our sinful nature.

Timothy will 'fan into flame' the gift of the Spirit as he boldly witnesses, relies on the Spirit's power rather than his own strength and intellect, sincerely loves as God loves, and shows the self-discipline that is a true mark of spiritual maturity.

Further Questions

1. What is the relationship between the Holy Spirit and the promise of life?

2. Is Paul being selfish in verse 4? What role does 'joy' have in living a faithful Christian life?

2 Timothy 1:8-14
A Herald and a Guardian

Key Truth: Timothy must follow the pattern set by Jesus and Paul, teaching and suffering for the gospel of life.

1. Suffer Without Shame (1:8)

The life of the great apostle Paul had been a life of suffering. Some of the Corinthian Christians had been ashamed of Paul's suffering and weakness. See 1 Corinthians 4:8-13, especially verses 9-10.

Bearing witness to Jesus will always be costly, always bring suffering, always be a denial of worldly glory and wisdom. The temptation is to see the apostles as unfortunate exceptions to the general rule of blessing and comfort. The temptation is to imagine that the glory we have in Jesus is to be experienced even now in this passing age. However, the sufferings of Jesus teach us that the Kingdom of God and the kingdom of this world are in head-on collision. We can only invest in one kingdom or the other. We cannot have the glory and esteem of **both** kingdoms. Jesus promised us that in this life we will have many troubles, yet we should not feel defeated because He has overcome the world (John 16:33). If Timothy tries to invest in **this** world, then he will be ashamed and barren in the age to come.

Timothy must embrace the wholehearted commitment to Jesus that Paul had displayed. Instead of trying to have an easy life, Timothy must join with Paul in suffering for the gospel by the power of God. This is the requirement of every Christian in every age and in every nation. It can only be done by the power of God. If we think about doing this in our own strength we will certainly give up and make selfish, comfortable choices. However, if we join with Jesus, Paul, Timothy – and Peter, Moses, David, Isaiah, Elijah, John the Baptist, yes, and the faithful Christians down the ages, we **will** know the power of God to sustain us through all our trials with great joy and peace.

Even now as you study these words, think about how you can claim more ground for the Kingdom of God in your life and witness. Where have you chosen comfort over faithfulness? Where have you been silent about Jesus when you should have spoken? Where have you been ashamed when you should have been bold?

2. Life and Immortality in Jesus (1:9–10)

We can be confident of the power of God in our weakness because the Father has already exercised this power to help our weaknesses in salvation. He saved us 'not because of anything we have done, but because of His own purpose and grace'.[1] We don't need to earn or deserve His help in living for Him. He has never dealt with us in such a way.

He saved us to call us to a **holy life**. Sometimes people think of holiness as an other-worldly kind of spirituality. We might think of holiness only in the negative – **not** worldly, **not** sinful, **not** compromised, etc. However, the Bible sees holiness in a much more positive way. Throughout the Hebrew Scriptures we see the word 'holy' attached to what is **set apart for the LORD's service**. It is about being dedicated to the Lord's use, rather than simply separate from the world. No matter how moral or religious a person is, if they are not dedicated to the Lord's service, they are not at all holy.

So, Paul reminds Timothy that in freely saving us, the Father saved us for a **holy** life – a life of usefulness dedicated to His service. This is why joining in the sufferings of Jesus without shame is not an optional extra for monks, ministers and missionaries. It is the basic purpose of our salvation. A Christian who is worldly has denied the very purpose of their salvation. There is only shame and dishonour in such a life.

But, we might ask, how can we be sure of this purpose? Such a life – a life where we crucify our fleshly desires for the service of the gospel – will demand our all. How can we know God **will** sustain us in this? How can we know that it will all be worth it? Can we have complete **confidence** in the grace of God through the **shameful** death of Jesus? How can we remain unashamed of following Jesus into His suffering?

---

[1] We must always be clear that Paul's challenge to Timothy has nothing to do with earning salvation. Paul never thinks for a single moment that Timothy's salvation depends on the level of sacrifice and commitment in his ministerial life. NO! Salvation is given to us freely as we simply trust in Jesus. Paul's challenge is on the basis of **living out** what we have already been freely given in Jesus. Throughout this letter he challenges Timothy to be true and faithful to this free grace in Jesus.

Before the world began, the crucifixion of Jesus was established as the very foundation of God's grace towards us (verse 9, and in Revelation 13:8). God's grace is not based on our works, but on His atoning death for us. So, Timothy must never be ashamed of the sufferings of Jesus, or the sufferings of His saints, or of the gospel message. These realities take us to the very foundation of the universe before any of us existed, before anyone had done anything good or bad. These truths are not to be apologised for but announced with utter joy and confidence. If we really understand this and embrace it then we will live it out in our daily lives.

Hebrews 11 describes how the Old Testament saints pursued the life that Paul is describing. However, Timothy has even more reason to be confident, because the Messiah came **as promised** and did all that was prophesied about Him. He really did destroy death and He really did show us what immortal, resurrection life looks like (verse 10).

Luke 10:23–24 tells us that Jesus told His disciples that many prophets and kings wanted to see what they see but did not see it, and hear what they hear but did not hear it. Again, in 1 Peter 1:10–12, we read that the prophets longed to see the sufferings and glories of Christ that they spoke about by the Spirit of Christ. However, this eternal grace of God in Jesus was manifested in His death and resurrection. Now, we have seen what they looked forward to.

Timothy has seen that the sufferings of Jesus led to the resurrection life of Jesus, just as planned and promised by the Father from the beginning of the world. The apostles actually saw with their own eyes what the promise of resurrection life looks like. Timothy knows that laying down his life for the gospel will yield eternal fruit because he has seen that in Jesus' own death and resurrection.

3. Paul Suffers Without Shame (1:11–12)

Paul has spent his life practising what he preaches. He doesn't ask Timothy to do anything that he has not already done.

Paul was appointed personally by Jesus to be 'a herald and an apostle and a teacher' of this glorious, eternal gospel (Galatians 1:11–12). Whereas he was the last of the apostles, yet the work of being a herald of the gospel is shared by every believer and the office of Bible teacher exists in every local church fellowship.

Apostle	Paul
Teacher	Paul, Timothy and every minister and pastor
Herald	Paul and every other believer

4. 'He Guards... You Guard' (1:12–14)

Paul is not disappointed by the gospel in spite of all the suffering it has brought on him. Paul sees reality. The Day of Judgement is approaching and the most important issue we all face is how we will stand before Jesus the Living God on that day. The gospel is the answer to that most urgent concern. Yet, it is not simply a matter of information. Paul says 'I know **WHOM** I have believed...' not 'I know **what** I have believed...'. There is a vital difference between these two. The gospel is essentially not a matter of information but a **relationship**. As James observes, the demons know it all to be true and they tremble, but it has no further impact on them. The gospel is not a mere belief that certain things really happened. The great joy and confidence of the Christian is **knowing Jesus**.

Paul knows Jesus, which gives him the complete confidence that he will be welcomed by Jesus on 'that day'. Paul has trusted Jesus to **guard** his own eternal safety, his body, soul and spirit. Faith in Jesus is entrusting Jesus with the sole care of our life, death and everlasting safety.[2]

If Jesus is the only One able to guard us on that day, then it is absolutely vital that the truth is **guarded** and passed on with the utmost care. If the corruption of the gospel means that people do not get to know Jesus then they will perish when they stand before Him. Therefore, Paul gives to Timothy the urgent and soul-saving task of guarding the gospel of Jesus.

Paul here speaks of a pattern, or more literally, 'a brief outline' of the sound teaching that he has taught Timothy. Timothy needs to have an outline of the gospel truth that will guide his own thinking and speaking. Richard Bewes often speaks of the four key features of our worldview. We might imagine how Paul might express this outline, from his letters.

Creation	Colossians 1:15–17	The whole creation is from the Father through and for Jesus
Fall	Romans 5:12–19; Ephesians 2:1–3	Through Adam's sin we are all dead in sin, enslaved to Satan and full of evil desires
Redemption	Romans 5:1–11; Romans 6:1–14	Jesus' death takes away our sin and His resurrection gives us a new life in the Spirit, free from the slavery of sin
Consummation	Romans 8:18–25	When Jesus returns He will judge the world, liberate the whole creation and give us immortal bodies

---

[2] There is another possibility for these words of Paul. It is quite possible that Paul is referring to his own apostolic ministry. Paul sees all the opposition to the true gospel, but he has entrusted this work to Jesus who will keep the gospel safe right until the end. Jesus certainly has done this, in spite of the many false teachers and heresies that have threatened to destroy the apostolic teaching.

It is not enough for Timothy to simply know these truths. He must guard them 'with faith and love in Christ Jesus'. He must trust and love Jesus if he is to keep the outline of truth safely. The way that he keeps the gospel is as important as the truth of it.

Timothy then must see himself as the guardian of the most precious of all treasures. However, he is not working alone. Standing with him is the mighty Holy Spirit. He is the supreme guardian and witness of Jesus. As Timothy seeks the help of this divine gospel guardian, so he will be able to face and overcome all challenges.

Further Questions

1. Can a person follow Jesus but dislike Paul? Why, or why not?

2. What is the relationship between suffering, weakness and power?

3. Is it ever right to say that Paul was 'a man of his time'? Why might some say this?

2 Timothy 1:15–2:14
Desertion and Endurance

Key Truth: For Timothy to bear fruit and eternal glory, he must work hard by God's grace and keep passing the gospel on to others.

1. 'Everyone' Deserted Me (1:15)

Verse 15 is one of the saddest verses in the New Testament – 'You know that everyone in the province of Asia has deserted me'. When we think how Paul poured out his life for the gospel in that area, it is terrible that as he prepares to die he feels so betrayed.

We don't know much about Phygelus and Hermogenes except that they were once fellow workers with Paul in Asia. Why did they turn away? If we are to judge by the advice given to Timothy, it would seem to be that they either were not prepared to suffer for the gospel and/or they did not guard the gospel outline properly. Whether they repented of their faithlessness or not, they have passed into history in the rogues' gallery. They stand as a sorry warning to us all. This letter of 2 Timothy is a heart-felt impassioned plea from the apostle Paul to Timothy (and every generation of minister) to follow his example rather than the fruitless, harmful, selfish example of Phygelus and Hermogenes.

2. Mercy to the Merciful (1:16–18)

Onesiphorus and his whole household were still faithful guardians of the gospel. He stands as a model for Timothy to follow. What a great joy his visit must have been to Paul while he was in prison!

We are reminded of Jesus' teaching in Matthew 25:31–46. Jesus had promised His disciples that they would suffer imprisonment, suffering and rejection (Matthew 10:16–28). In Matthew 25 Jesus teaches that the mark of being a genuine sheep in His flock is caring for our fellow Christians who are suffering for their gospel faithfulness. Whether we lose our jobs, our families, our money, our freedom, even our lives, we will find comfort and support through all these sufferings from the genuine followers of Jesus. The people who pretend to follow Jesus will be shown up as they desert us at these times.

3. Be Strong, Endure, Compete and Work Hard (2:1–6)

Paul is passing on the responsibility now to Timothy. Paul has stood firm in Jesus: now it is Timothy's turn. Paul sees himself and his co-workers as soldiers in a war situation. It is a vital mind-set to have. During a time of peace, a civilian may live as they please, free to pursue their own agenda. However, a soldier in a war cannot do that. It is absolutely essential that they carry out the orders of their commanding officer, or else they endanger not only themselves but also their fellow soldiers. The soldier will put up with harsh living conditions in order to fulfil his duties. Timothy must see himself as a soldier under Jesus' command with the same obedience, discipline and readiness to endure hardship that is demanded in a human army.

If Timothy sees his life in this way, then he will not expect to drift through life in comfort and ease. How are we living our lives? Are we spending our time, energy and money trying to live in a 'comfortable bedroom', or are we using all our resources for the gospel campaign? Do we obey Jesus only as He fits into our lifestyle and desires, or do we obey Him with the whole-hearted urgency of the good soldier? We may use our time in all kinds of activities which are perfectly innocent in themselves, but if they are distracting us from the work of Bible reading, prayer, witnessing, caring and teaching then we must push them away from us as if they were poison. Hebrews 12:1 – 'let us throw off **everything** that hinders'.

The next image Paul puts before Timothy is that of a dedicated athlete training for and competing in the games. We have perhaps heard how a professional athlete will get up early each morning to begin their hours of training. Every meal is planned to make sure that they have just the right nutrients for their effort. Every aspect of their life becomes focussed on the goal of being the champion, the gold medal winner. Anything less than this effort and commitment will never get them onto the winner's podium. During the contest itself they are not free to follow their own rules or invent their own challenge. The rules of the contest are clearly known and any competitor that breaks these rules will be disqualified. So, Timothy must have the same level of dedication and care in his own ministry. It is not that Timothy is trying to win the prize of salvation, but that he must give himself heart and soul to the work of the gospel if he is to be a fruitful, unashamed servant of Jesus.[3]

The final image is of a hard-working farmer who keeps on going – through heat and cold, through long hours of exhausting effort because he wants to reap the harvest. The farmer cannot just please himself or only work in the comfortable times. His work requires him to get up early and stay up late, to keep going in pouring rain, freezing cold and scorching heat. If he does not do this his crop will be overgrown with weeds, eaten by animals and yield a meagre result. This same tough-mindedness is required from the Christian minister.

In each image it is the end result that drives the person forward. The soldier for the approval of his officer, the athlete for the gold medal and the farmer for the final crop. Timothy must also set his vision on the time when he stands before Jesus on that day. If he has run the race, fought the fight and produced a fruitful harvest, Jesus will welcome him with the words 'well done, good and faithful servant'. All the effort, all the suffering, all the discipline, all the self-denial will then be counted as nothing compared to the wonders that surround him.

4. Reflect, Remember and Remind (2:7-14)

In these verses, Paul gives Timothy three basic commands: reflect, remember and remind.

First, Timothy must **reflect** on Paul's challenge to live a disciplined life of hardship. At first he might find it too much to bear, too harsh, too demanding. Perhaps he might suspect that Paul is overstating the effort required. However, Paul recommends that he **reflect** on these things. Think them through carefully. If he does this the Lord Jesus will show him the truth and wisdom of Paul's instructions.

If we reflect on the lives of all the saints in the Bible, from Noah down to Paul, we see them displaying the qualities that Paul describes. If they were to be useful to the Lord then they had to live the life of disciplined, dedicated hardship. How did they do it? Hebrews 11:13–16 explains. They set their vision on the **final goal** – life in the New Creation with the Father, Son and Holy Spirit. They made the hard choices that fruitfulness needs because they knew what was finally worthwhile.

Next, Timothy must **remember**. He must not simply remember information, but remember **Jesus**. If Jesus is at the centre of Timothy's heart and mind, he will see the truth of all this. Jesus is the One who inherits the

---

[3] Timothy is assured of salvation, but how will he be received at the appearing of Jesus? Will he be ashamed or will he receive a crown of honour?

everlasting Kingdom promised to David, and Jesus has been raised from the dead. These two facts encapsulate the great hope that we have in Jesus – eternal life and the everlasting Kingdom of God. What do we have now that can be compared to such a glorious future?

Paul is so identified with this faith and hope in Jesus that he calls it 'my gospel'. He does not just serve Jesus in his spare time or once a week. Even though this work has brought him to prison in Rome, Paul is consoled by the fact that the gospel itself is not chained. Whether he lives or dies, is imprisoned or free, rich or poor, loved or hated, Paul's only concern is for the freedom of the gospel of Jesus.

Verses 10–14 form a block. Is Paul speaking here of his evangelistic ministry to the unbelieving world? There are many excellent Bible commentators who take that view. From this viewpoint, the following verses are a warning that Jesus cannot ignore the warnings He has already given about those who refuse Him, and will certainly condemn to Hell anyone who denies Him.[4]

However, my own view is that his concern here is with the choice lying before Timothy and those Timothy will teach: **the choice between fruitfulness and barrenness**. The people spoken of in verse 14 seem to be the very same people spoken of here in these verses – the Christians that Timothy is ministering to, rather than the unbelieving world. It seems to me that Paul is continuing the theme that has been running from the beginning of this chapter.

Paul has seen how people started well in following Jesus, but became fruitless because they refuse to follow Him in the way of suffering and self-denial. He demonstrates this by reference to what may well have been a hymn used in the churches of the time, verses 11–13.

He begins with the foundation stone: our union with Jesus in His death and resurrection. If we are joined to Christ in His atoning death, then we are also born again (see Romans 6) and we will certainly also be joined to Him on the Day of Resurrection. If that is the foundation truth about us, we **must** live it out.

Now, can we lose our salvation? Can we be united to Jesus in His death and resurrection and yet end up being in Hell after the Day of Judgement? If we live unfaithful Christian lives, will we finally be lost? It is my view that verse 13 answers that question. Even if we are faithless, yet Jesus remains faithful. We are His own body and He will not disown Himself. Paul uses this striking phrase to underline the impossibility of any person united to Jesus in His death ever being lost. However, if our Christian lives are a denial of what we really are, lives that deny the way of the

---

[4] See William Hendriksen's commentary on 2 Timothy for an excellent presentation of this view.

Cross, then Jesus will not be pleased with us when we stand before Him to give an account of ourselves. Paul teaches this same truth in 1 Corinthians 3:11–15. Jesus may also disown our ministry here and now if we refuse to honour Him in it. The Lord will not bless a ministry that denies Him and brings no glory to Jesus, and in this way He will disown us.

So, in verses 10–14 Paul sets this sober reality before Timothy. His ministerial work will face the revealing fire of Jesus on the Day of Judgement. Will Jesus deny Timothy's work, or will Timothy receive a reward for his work? If Timothy's life as a Bible teacher is a denial of all that Paul has charged him with, Timothy would be saved because of the faithfulness of Jesus, but what a wasted life he will have lived.

There is a song I often used to sing when I was growing up and it has been echoing round my head as I have studied these words of Paul. It contains these lines: By and by when I look on His face, I'll wish I had given Him more.

Timothy must set this challenging truth before the Christians he must minister to. 'Keep **reminding** them of these things' (verse 14). It is not enough for him to mention them once, because we tend to drift away into the slumber of worldliness unless our future hope is constantly held before us.

Paul isolates the specific issue of worthless debates and arguments here. It is so easy for us, in our passion for truth, to spend endless amounts of time analysing the minutiae of our respective theological opinions and perspectives. In doing this we might imagine we are doing something worthwhile, but here Paul gives us the honest truth. When we consider the images of soldiers, athletes and farmers, we can see his point clearly. The soldier who spends his time debating with his friends during the conflict, the athlete who spends more time talking about sport than doing it, or the farmer who prefers magazine articles about weeding rather than actually weeding his crops would all be useless exponents of their professions.

This teaching from Paul wakes us all up. We might slumber in the belief that we may as well just live a quiet life until we get to paradise. Paul shakes us awake with the knowledge of the revealing fire that our lives must pass through on that final day. Will we be ashamed on that day? Or will we welcomed and rewarded for our suffering faithfulness?

Further Questions

1. Is training the role of Bible/Theological colleges, or local church leaders?

2. What is the relationship between Jesus being descended from David and the resurrection (see also Acts 2:22–36 and Romans 1:1–4)?

2 Timothy 2:15-3:9
Correctly Handling the Word of Truth

Key Truth: False teaching and godless living is deadly and can only be countered as Timothy flees evil and pursues the Biblical faith and lifestyle.

1. Godly and Ungodly Speakers (2:15-18)

Paul focuses now upon the kind of teaching that must characterise the fruitful ministry of Timothy. What must be built on the foundation of Jesus if it is to withstand the revealing fires of the final day?

He uses a fourth image – the workman. The material that this 'workman' works with is the Bible. The master craftsman who will inspect his work is none other than God the Father. Timothy must put all his effort into being the very best Bible-workman that he can possibly be. If he does not want to be ashamed on that final day when his work is inspected, then he must be utterly dedicated to his craft.

The craft is correctly handling the Word of truth. How is this done? John Stott expresses the task of the Bible teacher so well. We must 'be accurate on the one hand and plain on the other in our exposition'.[5]

Being a God-approved Bible teacher doesn't just happen by accident. It comes about as the minister spends hour after hour, day after day, week after week, year after year reading, learning, analysing, comparing and studying the words of Scripture. The study of the Bible **must** always be the top ministry priority for any minister, or else all the other tasks (however worthy and useful) will fill up the time and energy. Do you read the Bible through at least once a year? Do you understand the 'storyline' of the whole Bible?[6] Can you explain the common issues of life from the Bible?

---

[5] John Stott, BST, page 67
[6] 'God's Big Picture' by Vaughan Roberts (IVP)

Positively, Timothy must speak the words of Scripture, but negatively, he must avoid godless chatter (verse 16). When Paul says this he is referring to false teaching, the kind of harmful speculations, philosophical dogmas and unbelieving opinion that destroys lives. He refers to it as 'gangrene' (verse 17) because its corruption spreads and grows. A minister might think that he can be a little unorthodox about one or two subjects, but godless teaching cannot be contained and controlled in this way. Once the authority of the Bible is surrendered there is no way to prevent the influx of false ideas.

Hymenaeus and Philetus are held up as examples of this spreading and destructive process. He describes them as 'wandering' away from the truth, as if it has happened by default, as if they had simply lost the focus of where they were going. The flesh is always warring against the Spirit (Galatians 5), and if we are not consciously and deliberately walking in step with the Spirit we will inevitably and increasingly be controlled by the flesh. False teaching is against God and against humanity. It does not only offend the Lord God, but it also corrupts and destroys human lives. It is one of the cruellest of all crimes.

2. God's Foundation (2:19)

We might be worried that the entire Church could be destroyed by false teaching. Paul reassures us that God's solid foundation stands firm. What is this foundation? Isaiah 28:16 tells us that the 'sure foundation' that will never let anyone down is Jesus the Messiah.[7] If we are built on that firm foundation we cannot be moved.

Jesus told us how to identify the false teacher – 'by their fruit you will know them' (Matthew 7:15–20). The Lord always knows the true from the false and as this is inevitably shown in action, so we must have nothing to do with false teachers.

Paul here quotes Numbers 16:5 and 26 as they appear in the Greek translation of the Hebrew Scriptures. It is such a good Biblical reference to warn us about godless chatter. Numbers 16 is the story of Korah's rebellion. Some Sabbath-breakers were put to death (Numbers 15:32–36) according to the LORD's instruction. Korah and his friends, Dathan and Abiram, felt that this was too much. They challenge Moses' leadership. However, to oppose Moses was nothing less than opposing the choice and words of the LORD. So, Moses says, 'the LORD knows who are His... He will show who belongs to Him and who does not'. All

---

[7] See Matthew 21:42; Acts 4:11; 1 Corinthians 3:11; Ephesians 2:20; Romans 9:33, 10:11 and 1 Peter 2:8.

those standing with Korah and his men, including those members of their families who would not leave them behind, were swallowed up by the earth.[8]

Paul's reference to this story is so illuminating. The false teachers may appear to be part of the Church family. However, their godless chatter and unbiblical teaching will show them up for what they are. We must have nothing to do with anyone like that, because if we don't get away from them, their destructive words will bring harm on us as well.

Paul knows that Timothy belongs to Jesus. The choice that Paul is constantly putting before him is not so much Heaven or Hell, but a fruitful, approved entrance into the New Creation or a barren, ashamed entrance into the New Creation. This is the choice that every Christian minister or home group leader needs to come back to every day.

3. Godly Living (2:20–26)

Timothy knows what he must **teach** in order to be fruitful, but what kind of a life must he **live**?

Paul turns to another vivid image. This time (verses 20–21) we are considering a large house with all kinds of different articles – some are honoured and some are dishonoured; some are very precious to the master of the house, whereas others are good only for very basic and trivial purposes.

We find this image of the Church as a house in 1 Timothy 3:15; 1 Peter 2:5, 4:17. This seems to indicate that Paul is speaking here of the different kinds of lives that Christians may lead – lives of holiness that please the Lord or lives of worldliness that displease Him. There is nothing fixed about these two categories. Paul says that any Christian can become useful for noble purposes if he will cleanse himself from dishonourable activities. He can be 'made holy, useful to the Master, and prepared to do any good work'. Now Paul explains what that means in greater detail in verses 2:22–3:9.

First, Timothy is to **flee** and **pursue**. The temptation is to think that we can have a little bit of our favourite sin without any real harm. We imagine we can tolerate our materialism, our love of comfort, our pride, our love of wealth, our lust, our anger, our cowardice, our gossip or grumbling. Scripture tells us the honest truth – if we do not **flee** from all our sin

---

[8] It is interesting to note that some of Korah's sons **did** separate from him, because some of the Psalms are written by the Sons of Korah. (See Psalms 42, 44–49, 84–85, 87–88)

it will harm us, reduce our usefulness and lead us to be a vessel of merely 'ignoble purposes'.

However, on the other hand, Timothy is told to **pursue** righteousness, faith, love and peace in godly company. It's a wonderful image – the Christian fellowship using its energies to hunt down and capture righteous living – more trust in Jesus, more sincere love and deeper peace with each other.

From verses 24–26 Paul gives another perspective on how Timothy may cleanse himself from 'ignoble purposes', specifically in the matter of argument. Because every Bible teacher is 'the LORD's servant' he has no need to be quarrelsome. He is not defending his own ideas or fighting for a merely human ideology. It is the LORD's Word and He can defend it perfectly well on His own. So, the minister can be at peace, knowing that the truth and power of the Word will not be harmed by the unbelief of anybody we come across.

When opposed, the Bible teacher must 'gently instruct' (verse 25), patiently hoping that the Father will open eyes to the truth. The teacher is not so gentle that he gives into error, but will always respond to error with 'gentle instruction'.

The person who opposes the teaching of the Bible might think themselves 'open-minded' and 'liberated'. However, according to verse 26 they are in the trap of the devil, enslaved to do his will, out of their senses. How can they get out? They don't have the power to free themselves, so they must be gently instructed in the hope that God will rescue them from their satanic slavery.

4. The Form of Godliness (3:1– 9)

Now by way of contrast Paul gives a more detailed account of false teachers. It is as if Paul finds it best to show Timothy how he **should** be by carefully showing all that he **shouldn't** be.

Timothy will encounter this ocean of sinfulness **within the Church**. The real danger is not that the unbelieving world lives an unbelieving life, but that the Church might begin to do that due to the false teachers within it. 'Two traitors within the garrison may do more hurt to it than two thousand besiegers without' (Matthew Henry).

Such people are not content to quietly exist within the Church. Their hatred of the Lord means that they desire to make the Church in their own image, as a place of darkness and sin. Therefore, verse 6, they 'worm their way into homes'. They are not honest about their intentions. They try to find those who are most vulnerable in the fellowship, or those who are weighed down with sin and evil desires. If a Christian will flee evil

Lovers of themselves	This the root of all sin. We take the place of Jesus in our hearts and minds	Genesis 3:1–7
Boastful	Boasting always follows self-love. It is excluded by the gospel	Psalm 10:3; Romans 3:27; 1 Corinthians 1:26–31
Proud	The original sin of Satan	1 Timothy 3:6; Isaiah 14:12–14; Ezekiel 28:17
Abusive	The opposite of Jesus	1 Peter 2:21–23
Disobedient to their parents	The way we treat our parents reflects our view of our heavenly Father	Romans 1:30; Colossians 3:20; Ephesians 6:1
Ungrateful	Gratitude is how we respond to God's grace	Psalm 75:1; 105:1
Unholy	We are saved to be holy just as the Lord is holy	1 Peter 1:15; 2 Timothy 1:9
Without love	Plenty of love for self and pleasure, but no **real** love	1 Corinthians 13
Unforgiving	The believer forgives others just as they have been forgiven	Matthew 18:21–35; 6:9–15
Slanderous	The devil always brings false accusations. To follow him is to share his character	Revelation 12:20
Without self-control	Self-control is a fruit of the Spirit not the flesh	Galatians 5:22
Brutal	The way that Jesus was murdered reveals the sinful human heart. Violent films are considered entertaining	Isaiah 53:3, 7–9
Not lovers of the good	If we love the Lord we hate evil. If we do not love goodness, we hate the Lord	Amos 5:14–15; Psalm 97:10
Treacherous	Judas' betrayal was far from being a unique sin. To put money, comfort, or anything over our love of the Lord and each other is the seed-bed of treachery	Matthew 26:14–16
Rash	The book of Proverbs is full of examples of the foolishness of acting without thinking	Proverbs 1:1–7
Conceited	To be wise in your own eyes is utter foolishness to the Living God	Proverbs 26:12; James 3:13–17; 1 Corinthians 1:18–25
Lovers of pleasure rather than lovers of God	It is not that pleasure is loved **more** than God, but that God is not loved **at all**	John 3:19; 12:43

desires and take the Word of truth to heart, then they are not going to be taken in by these deceitful corrupters. The Christian who lives a compromised and worldly life is utterly vulnerable to false teachers.

Paul gives the example of Jannes and Jambres who opposed Moses.[9] The name Jannes means 'one who answers back' and the name Jambres means 'one who opposes, a rebel'. It might be possible that Paul is simply speaking of the same incident in Numbers 16 that he has just referred to. He could be talking about Korah's two friends, Dathan and Abiram, who, with Korah, led the opposition against Moses – 'Just as the Opposer and the Rebel opposed Moses in Numbers 16, so also these false Christians oppose the truth'.

Once again Paul reassures Timothy that their true character cannot be hidden. Timothy must be on his guard and make sure that the whole Church family is on their guard against this kind of person. It will be a common feature of life until Jesus returns. When we identify such a person in the Church family it is vital that we exercise the proper Church discipline and have nothing to do with them. We dare not tolerate them among us or else they will destroy 'the faith of some'.

---

[9] Jewish legends say that these could be the names of the magicians who opposed Moses in Exodus 7:11, 22; 8:7, 18–19.

Further Questions

1. How much of the New Testament is written to combat or expose false teaching? What does this teach us?

2. Is it ok to receive communion from a false teacher? Why or why not?

3. With verse 19 in mind, is it right to question whether someone is or is not a Christian? If it is right, how should this be done?

2 Timothy 3:10-4:8
Scriptures and Preaching

Key Truth: In view of Christ's appearing, Timothy's priority must be to teach the Bible, despite rejection and persecution, because only in this way will people be saved and
equipped for a godly life.

1. 'My Teaching, My Way of Life' (3:10-13)

'YOU, however...' It is an arresting beginning to Paul's next charge to
Timothy. He must not follow the example of the compromised Christians
or the false teachers. He has a much better example right before him: the
life of the apostle Paul. Whereas the false leaders always try to conceal
what they are up to, Timothy knows all about Paul's life and teaching
(verse 10).

Before Paul describes his life and purpose, he mentions his teaching.
The engine behind Paul's life was the 'Word of truth'. Our lives are determined by what we believe, by what we cherish, by what we value. If Timothy is to live like Paul he must believe and teach like Paul.

Timothy had been an apprentice to the great apostle, and now it was
time for Timothy to live out for himself all that he had learned from Paul.
If he did this, Timothy would never need to be ashamed before Jesus. Yes,
it is a hard task (verse 12), but the joy, peace and divine fellowship that
Paul had known would also belong to Timothy.

Isn't there another alternative? Can't I follow Jesus in a comfortable
way? No, and in verse 13 Paul gives us the only other option: 'evil men
and impostors will go from bad to worse, deceiving and being deceived'.
Whether we are an outright pagan or a person pretending to follow
Jesus, we end up the same way – going from bad to worse. Even if we are
a believer in Jesus, if we avoid the conflict and hard work that the gospel
brings, we will never live a godly life.

2. The Purpose of the Hebrew Scriptures (3:14–17)

'But as for **you**…' Paul doesn't contemplate the possibility that Timothy will not want to live a godly life in Christ Jesus. Rather, Timothy is on the right track. Since he was an infant he was instructed in the Scriptures (surely one of the very greatest blessings it is possible to receive![10]) and had been Paul's apprentice in more recent years. He had seen the godliness of his mother, his grandmother and the apostle Paul. Timothy knew that the truth they had taught him was the **real thing**.

Paul isolates Timothy's instruction in the Scriptures as being the firm foundation for his whole ministry (verses 15–16). He was speaking here only of the Hebrew Scriptures, but the same truths apply also to the Greek Scriptures that we have in addition.

What is the purpose of the Scriptures? To make us wise for salvation through faith in Christ Jesus. John Calvin said: 'The Scriptures should be read with the aim of finding Christ in them. Whoever turns aside from this object, even though he wears himself out all of his life in learning, he will never reach the knowledge of the truth'.[11]

Timothy must be crystal clear on this. The Scriptures were **breathed-out** by God so that we would believe in Jesus the promised Messiah. In verse 16 Paul tells us that all the Scriptures are produced by God the Spirit – the Breath of God. This is vital to know, because the work of the Spirit is to bear witness to Jesus, to direct attention only to Jesus (John 16:5–15). In 1 Peter 1:11 we see that when the Spirit produced the Hebrew Scriptures, He was pointing to the sufferings and glories of Jesus the promised Messiah.

The areas of usefulness that Paul isolates fulfil all the needs that he has set before Timothy: teaching, rebuking, correcting, training in righteousness. This must be remembered when we think about ministerial training. The Bible alone can comprehensively equip a minister for every pastoral challenge.

3. Preach the Word (4:1–5) (cf. 2:1–6)

What a sobering and solemn charge verse 1 is! It may well be that Paul was just days away from his death and therefore these would have been the very last words that he ever wrote. His profound charge to Timothy, by the Spirit's power and direction, echoes down to every church leader

---

[10] It is disturbing when Christian parents work so hard to give their children 'the best opportunity' in life, yet put so much less effort into training them in the Scriptures.

[11] John Calvin, 'The Gospel According to John', volume 2, page 139.

ever since. Surely these opening verses of 2 Timothy 4 must always be the words that are read to any and every minister as they begin their work.

Appealing to the very highest authority of all, Paul makes the job of the church leader as clear and simple as it could ever be – 'preach the word'. The temptation is to often allow other aspects of the minister's job to take the centre stage: administration of the sacraments, visitation, social action, etc. However, at the heart and foundation of every church leader must be preaching the Word. Only **this** can safeguard and guide the other activities.

Preach the Word	This is the overall heading for the work of any and every church leader. There are different styles of preaching, but only one ultimate method – faithfully explaining the original meaning of the Bible.
Be prepared	If we are going to be fruitful and faithful church leaders, then we must put lots of time into the work **in advance**. The Spirit is just as much at work in our preparation as in our delivery.
In season and out of season	In each age, in each situation, there are many parts of the Bible that people will not want to hear, or will want to explain away. There are many situations in which it will be extremely difficult to speak the truth about Jesus. We must never be belligerent or rude, but we must always speak that divine Word whether it is popular or unpopular.
Correct	Paul has spoken about the many errors that will always threaten the Church. If Timothy faithfully preaches the Word at all times, then these errors can be corrected. This is the positive aspect of the Word – showing the correct way against errors.
Rebuke	Preaching the Word also has a negative aspect – pointing out what is wrong, highlighting the errors. This is just as vital to us. A local church that hears the divine Word week-by-week is able to recognise false teachers quickly and avoid their life-destroying errors.
Encourage	Our loving Father's marvellous Word, by the power of the Spirit, can encourage and sustain us through all we must face. There is nothing so uplifting in trouble as hearing the glorious truths of the Bible.
With great patience	A passion for truth has sometimes been unfortunately coupled with harshness and impatience. We are helpless sinners and our Heavenly Father always treats us with miraculous patience and love. This must be reflected in the manner of His church leaders.
And careful instruction	Sometimes people divide Bible teaching from pastoral care. We must resist this. All our encouraging, rebuking and correcting must flow out of our 'careful instruction'.

The divine Word is liberating truth, but because of the corrupting power of sin humanity would prefer to listen to something else – anything else (verses 3–4). One of the symptoms of the disease of sin is 'itching ears' and we scratch this itch by listening only to the words we **want** rather than the truth we **need**.

Paul shows us a frightening truth about the human race. Far from being objective we will look for the teachers that suit our own desires. 'They do not first listen and then decide whether what they have heard is true; they first decide what they want to hear and then select teachers who will oblige by toeing their line'.[12] When we sin, we prefer to hear someone tell us we are 'a victim of a low self-value' or 'trapped by wrongs done to us earlier in life'. If someone can excuse our sin, our itching ears will want to listen to them. Maybe we prefer a teacher who will tell us that our sins are actually virtues. We will always be able to find somebody who will find a way around the Bible's teaching, who will 'affirm' our selfish desires, telling us that we are 'just enjoying the good things that God has given'. A teacher who will cater to the sinful itching ears of humanity will always have a popular following. The only remedy for this is the hard-work of Bible teaching that tells **God's** truth whether we desire it or not, especially as it challenges our sinful desires.

Paul specifies that Timothy must 'do the work of an evangelist'. In my experience this is what is most likely to disappear from a church's agenda. Evangelism is always hard work and requires self-sacrifice. We will always be 'too busy' for such work and it will never be the right time in the life of our local church. We will always feel that we need to do more training, more preparation, more planning. **However**, evangelism is the reason for the Church's existence in the world. Telling others about Jesus is the most loving, most important thing we can ever do for them. It is amazing how often a leader will say 'but that is just not my gift'. If that is the case, the Holy Spirit seems to have been rather unwise in giving this gift out so extremely rarely! Whether we have a special gift for the work or not, it is part of the basic work of any church leader. Timothy must fulfil all his duties, but Paul singles out the work of evangelism to keep it always high on the agenda.

4. Keep the Faith (4:6–8)

In these verses Paul is transferring his work onto Timothy. Paul is so near to the end of his life that he speaks of it as already completed, and (verse 8) he knows that he has no need to be ashamed on the day when Jesus

---

[12] John Stott, BST, page 111

returns. His faithful and fruitful life will not be burned up in the presence of Jesus. Paul returns to the images of a soldier and an athlete of chapter 2. He has done just what he has charged Timothy to do.

In verse 6 Paul refers us to his life as a drink offering. A drink offering involved pouring out wine, either on its own, or more usually over an animal sacrifice. The Scriptures frequently connect wine and blood[13] and Leviticus 17:11–14 tells us that the **life** of a creature is in its blood. So, we find that a drink offering is used to indicate a life dedicated to the Lord's service.[14]

Now, in 2 Timothy 4:6–8 Paul is looking back at his life as completed and now he pours out his life as a final statement that all his time and energy has been given over to the Lord Jesus. He has not run or laboured for nothing.

Paul concludes by challenging Timothy to pursue the same life and receive the same reward. Paul's crown of righteousness is not for apostles only, but for every believer who pours out their life with their heart and mind fixed on the appearing of Jesus. Paul has made it abundantly clear to Timothy what his life must be like if he loves the appearing of Jesus… and any hardship that such a life brings will appear momentary and light compared to the glory of the Day of Jesus that will never be followed by night.

---

[13] For example, see Genesis 49:11; John 2:3–4; Luke 22:20; 1 Corinthians 11:25–27.
[14] See this also in Genesis 35, and Numbers 28–29.

Further Questions

1. Should Christianity and preaching ever be popular?

2. Can someone be a good pastor but not a good teacher?

3. How can we tell the difference between (a) preaching that uses the Bible but teaches myths and/or what people want to hear, and (b) the kind of preaching Paul has in mind?

2 Timothy 4:9-4:22
Friends and Families

Key Truth: Our choice is between temporary comfort in this world or aligning ourselves with Paul and proclaiming the Biblical gospel, with the strength and companionship of our Lord Jesus Himself.

1. Friends

Paul wanted fellowship in his final days. Just as Jesus strongly desired the fellowship of His disciples just before His death (Luke 22:15), so the apostle Paul feels the same eager desire for his Christian family, verse 9. Right back at the beginning of the letter Paul remembered how painful it had been to part from Timothy, presumably at the time of Paul's arrest, 1:4. Paul longs now for some final fellowship with this dearly loved young minister who was being charged with continuing the apostolic work in the next generation.

It has been commented that Paul shows weakness here because he should have been satisfied simply with the intimate fellowship that he had with Jesus by the Spirit. Although this might sound quite spiritual it is not true to Scripture. We only need to read Psalm 22 to see how desperately even Jesus longed for human friendship during His passion. Humanity was created in the image of God, the God who is a community of Three Persons. We were designed to depend on each other and look after each other.

As isolated as Paul might feel, yet he is not really alone. This chapter lists many of his co-workers who are still going on with the gospel work.

Tychicus was a close companion of Paul, and was with him in his first imprisonment. How valuable Tychicus would have been to Paul at this time, and yet the needs of the Ephesian Christians matter more to Paul than his own comfort, verse 12.

We know nothing more about Crescens than we learn in this verse – that he had gone to Galatia. Perhaps Paul has sent this co-worker to Galatia because he was concerned that they did not get taken captive again by 'another gospel' (Galatians 1:6–7).

We know a lot more about Titus. Not only does he have a whole letter addressed to him while he was still working in Crete, but we find him mentioned throughout Paul's letters. In 2 Corinthians 7 we see just how much he meant to Paul. Titus was a man who was able to comfort Paul... and yet it seems that Paul thought that Titus could be of more use to the gospel in Dalmatia than comforting the apostle in his final days.

In verse 11 we see that only Luke is still with Paul. Luke had chronicled the acts of the apostles, focussing mainly on the acts of the apostle Paul. He had been a travelling companion of Paul (see for example Acts 16:10–16; 20:5–15). It is good for us to know that Paul had at least this one faithful companion in his final days.

Paul specifically asks that Timothy would bring Mark. Mark is a great encouragement to us. On Paul's first missionary journey, Mark had deserted Paul (see Acts 15:35–40). They had such a sharp disagreement that they parted company. Barnabas took Mark and sailed for Cyprus, but Paul chose Silas and left, commended by the brothers to the grace of the Lord. However, this was not the end of John Mark's work. When Paul writes to the Colossians he has clearly seen better things in Mark, Colossians 4:10. He is described as a fellow-worker in Philemon verse 24, and it seems that the apostle Peter also worked with him (1 Peter 5:13).

Mark is such a wonderful encouragement because he had been restored to fruitfulness after his barren, ignoble time of deserting Paul. Many of us need to focus on the example of Mark. Many of us have made fruitless, wasteful choices with our lives. Many of us have deserted the cause of the gospel at different times. The example of John Mark tells us that we should not despair. Our desertion, sin and barrenness do not have to have the final word over our ministry. If we will accept the charge that Paul gives to Timothy then we can once again become a fellow-worker for noble work in the Lord's household.

In the apparently incidental remark of verse 13, we find some important truths. We know nothing more about Carpus, but it seems that Paul had left Troas in a hurry and had been unable to bring his scrolls and parchments with him. Presumably this was because he had been arrested at Troas.

Paul speaks here of 'books' and parchment rolls. Christians have always been passionate about literacy. One of the first effects of revival in 18th Century England was the desire to learn to read. The culture may be a 'non-book' culture, but in this the Church will always be counter-culture. We live our lives around a book, the Bible, and our great desire to understand and live out this Biblical faith generates more books. The Bible commands us to read the Scriptures every day (see Psalms 1 and 119).

At the very end of the letter (verses 19–21) Paul mentions a crowd of other Christians who he knew were remaining faithful to the gospel and fruitful service.

We have already noticed how faithful Onesiphorous had been, 1:16–18. Erastus is mentioned in Acts 19:22 when Paul had sent him to Macedonia. We now learn that he was working in Corinth. Trophimus was part of the apostolic party mentioned in Acts 20:4, but in Acts 21:29 we learn that he was a Gentile Ephesian whose presence in Jerusalem attracted plenty of hostility. The fact that here in 2 Timothy Paul says that he left him sick in Miletus reminds us that physical healing is not an essential aspect of the gospel as certain modern false teachers proclaim.

When Paul mentions the other names in verse 21, it shows us that there were Christians in Rome who were in contact with Paul. We may well ask why the Roman Church, to whom Paul had written such a wonderful manifesto for global evangelism, were not more supportive of Paul in his imprisonment? We can't answer that question, but we find here at least a hint that some of the Roman Church were meeting with Paul.

2. Failures

Paul criticises two men in these final verses. One was a man who had once been a fruitful minister of the gospel but had now become an ignoble or fruitless member of Christ's body and one was a man who was an enemy of the gospel, having no part in the body of Christ at all.

Demas deserted Paul in Rome and went to Thessalonica (verse 10). He did this because he 'loved this world'. If we read Acts 17:1–10 it is not clear why a Christian who 'loved this world' would make his way to Thessalonica! It did not seem to be the kind of place to go if you wanted an easy Christian life. However, if Paul was caught in Emperor Nero's persecution of the Christians then anywhere away from Rome might have been enough for Demas. We know that Demas was a Christian because earlier Paul had written well of him, Philemon 1:23–24, but now he had allowed the values and desires of **this** world to control him. We might well sympathise with Demas' cowardice, but Paul puts his finger on the real problem. Demas loved his own life and comfort more than he loved Jesus. He longed for life in this world more than he longed for the appearing of Jesus. In verse 17 we see that Paul does not want Demas to be judged for this, but it does indicate a problem in Demas' heart. How often have we seen this happen? How often have we seen a very promising Christian life become barren and pointless because of a love for this world? At the appearing of Jesus what will they be able to say to their Lord and Saviour?

Demas once loved Jesus more than this world, but Alexander the metalworker never loved Jesus at all. A more literal translation of verse 14 seems to indicate that Alexander had been an informer, spreading evil ideas about Paul, presumably to the Roman authorities. Is this why Paul had been arrested and imprisoned for this second time?

Alexander did more than simply cause personal problems for Paul, verse 15. The real danger of Alexander was his opposition to the gospel. The people who are the most dangerous are not the ones who cause us lots of personal problems (however inconvenient or painful they may be to us). The gravest, **eternal** danger is found in those who oppose the gospel itself, no matter how pleasant they may be to us. Paul solemnly predicts that the Lord will repay Alexander for what he has done.

3. Jesus Stood By Me

Paul may be referring to his first imprisonment in verse 16; however the context perhaps seems more likely to indicate a reference to his initial legal hearing in this second imprisonment. In his first imprisonment he did not seem to experience the isolation that he did now. Now he writes that 'everyone deserted me'. The fear of execution, whether by lions, the sword or crucifixion is certainly terrifying and although Paul makes it clear that the follower of Jesus must follow Him into such suffering, yet he writes 'may it not be held against them'.

Paul did not love **this** world. He longed only to be with Jesus, to invest in the **coming** world. When he speaks of being rescued 'from every evil attack' he was not thinking about escaping to Thessalonica, but escaping into paradise beyond death. The great rescue that we need is not the temporary rescue from pain, but the everlasting rescue from the torment of Hell.

Paul was facing death, perhaps being thrown to the lions in the arena (verse 17).[15] Paul's only concern is that he will faithfully proclaim the gospel even in this most 'out of season' occasion. He is thankful that Jesus stood with him and strengthened him. We can imagine Paul explaining the good news of Jesus even when he had been sentenced to death.

---

[15] It is unlikely however that a Roman citizen would have been thrown to the lions. It is perhaps more likely that 'the lion's mouth' refers either to Emperor Nero or the devil (see 1 Peter 5:8).

The last two verses of Charles Wesley's great hymn 'Jesus the Name high over all' summarise the final days of the great apostle Paul.

> His only righteousness I know
> His saving grace proclaim.
> 'Tis all my business here below,
> To cry behold the Lamb.
> Happy, if with my latest breath
> I can but gasp His name
> Preach Him to all and cry in death,
> Behold, behold the Lamb.

Verse 22: 'The Lord be with your spirit. Grace be with you'. The Lord Jesus stood by Paul, his greatest and unfailing Co-worker and Friend... now Paul wishes the reader to know the same unfailing Friend who will never desert us no matter what we might face.

Further Questions

1. If Luke was with Paul during his final days, why does Luke end the book of Acts with Paul's first imprisonment? Why didn't he write a second volume taking the biography of Paul right through to its conclusion?

2. Can Jesus be with us right now? What about the Father, or the Spirit? What does the Bible have to say about where each member of the Trinity is right now?